Till We Meet Again

A play

Colin and Mary Crowther

Samuel French — London
New York - Toronto - Hollywood

© 2002 BY COLIN CROWTHER AND MARY CROWTHER

Rights of Performance by Amateurs are controlled by Samuel French Ltd, 52 Fitzroy Street, London W1T 5JR, and they, or their authorized agents, issue licences to amateurs on payment of a fee. **It is an infringement of the Copyright to give any performance or public reading of the play before the fee has been paid and the licence issued.**

The Royalty Fee indicated below is subject to contract and subject to variation at the sole discretion of Samuel French Ltd.

Basic fee for each and every
performance by amateurs   Code E
in the British Isles

The publication of this play does not imply that it is necessarily available for performance by amateurs or professionals, either in the British Isles or Overseas. Amateurs and professionals considering a production are strongly advised in their own interests to apply to the appropriate agents for written consent before starting rehearsals or booking a theatre or hall.

ISBN 0 573 02360 3

Please see page iv for further copyright information

TILL WE MEET AGAIN

First performed on 7th April 2001 by The Players, Skelmersdale, at the All England Theatre Festival in the Gladstone Theatre, Port Sunlight.

CHARACTERS

Old Man, who plays Doctor, Manager, Grandad
Man, who plays himself between the ages of 30 and 45
Young Man, who plays himself as a teenager and as a
    man in his early 20s and also plays his successor at
    work and his neighbour
Old Woman, who plays Midwife, Grandmother, Cleaner,
    Senior Clerical Officer, Neighbour and herself
Woman, who plays Mother and Wife
Young Woman, who plays Sister, Junior Clerical Officer,
    Girlfriend, Nurse and Neighbour

The action of the play takes place somewhere between
heaven and earth

Playing time—45 minutes

SETTING

A bare stage allows a table, two chairs, a slatted wooden
bench and a sofa to represent an office, a kitchen, a bus
stop, an old people's home, a living-room, a hospital ...
and a place between heaven and earth

Other titles published by Samuel French Ltd:

By Colin Crowther

Footprints in the Sand

Tryst

By Colin and Mary Crowther:

Noah's Ark

This play is dedicated,
with the authors' grateful thanks,
to the Peggy Ramsay Foundation

TILL WE MEET AGAIN

When the CURTAIN *rises, four acting areas are lit. A kitchen is* RC, *simply represented by a table with two chairs. A park is* UC, *represented by a modern wheelchair and a low slatted wooden bench—which will later double as a coffee table. The wheelchair and bench are angled towards each other. A living-room is* LC, *represented by a sofa, angled away from us. A plain cotton throw-over is draped over the back of the sofa—this will later be opened up and used as a bed cover. The area from* C *to* DR *and* DL *is bare—the corridor between life and death. All the props in this play will be mimed. See ground plan on page 47*

Man is sprawled on the centre of the sofa, his legs splayed out on the floor, his head just visible over the back. Old Man, playing the part of Doctor, is kneeling below Man, taking his pulse. Doctor is aloof, untouched by events, conscious only of his power. Woman, now playing the part of Wife—tired, strained and numb—is standing US *at the back of the sofa, looking on. Doctor and Wife will normally be unaware of any interruptions to their conversation and carry on, silently where necessary, as if nothing untoward were happening*

In a neighbouring apartment, a young couple are about to eat a meal, Young Man sitting US *of the table, and Young Woman sitting* R *of the table, dishing out two huge platefuls of a very sticky attempt at macaroni cheese*

The actors are silhouetted against a bright glow from the cyc

They freeze as Old Woman enters DR, *as Midwife, pushing a forty-year-old pram to* DRC. *She is brisk, confident, chirpy*

Doctor rises

Doctor (*to Wife*) I'm sorry.
Midwife Now. Have I got everything?
Doctor Your husband…
Midwife Towels. Hot water.

Man rises very smoothly then turns sharply and looks back at "himself"

Doctor Naturally, we did all we could, but at his age…
Man I'm no age at all. I'm just turned forty.
Midwife (*absent-mindedly*) Forty-three.
Doctor But at his age…
Man What? What?
Doctor Fatal.
Midwife Fatal? (*She suddenly realizes she is witnessing a death, not a birth*) Oh dear. Got the wrong end of it again.
Man Rubbish. The man's a fool.
Wife Thank you, Doctor. (*She turns to face* US)

Man turns to his Wife but she cannot see him

Man (*to his Wife*) Don't listen to him. Send for someone else. I want a second opinion. (*He waves his hand in front of her face*) Hallo? Hallo? (*He crosses above and round her, pretending to knock on her head*) Anyone in? (*To Midwife*) I demand a second opinion.

Midwife pushes her pram up to RC

Midwife I don't know. Happens more and more these days.
Man Life begins at forty. Everyone knows that. (*He begins to cross to her*)
Midwife Or, in your case, ends. Well, I won't be needing this. (*She turns* DS *as if to push away the pram*)

Man grabs the pram

Man There's been a mistake. A terrible mistake.
Midwife Has there now? Well, I do get confused sometimes.

Doctor blows his nose on a huge but invisible handkerchief and puts it back in his breast pocket. Wife heaves a big sobbing sigh and turns DS. *Doctor passes her the handkerchief*

Doctor My deepest…
Midwife Wait for it.

Wife blows in the handkerchief, obliterating what Doctor was saying

Missed it.

Wife hands back the handkerchief. Doctor, reluctantly, puts it in his breast pocket

Wife Sorry.
Doctor No, no, it is I who am sorry.

But we suspect he is referring to the state of his handkerchief

Midwife That's no good. What we need is an action replay. (*She points a finger at them*)

Robotically, Doctor and Wife "rewind" their moves

Now—play.
Doctor My deepest——
Midwife This is it, this is it!
Doctor Condolences.

Repeat handkerchief business

Wife Sorry.
Doctor No, no, it is I who am sorry. (*He crosses slowly* DLC, *filling in the death certificate*)
Man He's got it wrong, wrong!
Midwife I'll ask. (*She steps towards Doctor*) Have you...?

Doctor comes round below the sofa, to DC, *still writing. He speaks without looking up*

Doctor No.
Midwife It has been known...
Doctor ...but never proved.
Midwife I only ask because——

They meet below the sofa

Doctor (*looking at Midwife*) Madam, do I look Chinese? I am not Chinese. If I were I should be paid only when my patients were well. Think of it. A few months of glorious sunshine and I should be out of a job. But I am not Chinese. Therefore, I am paid only when my patients are ill. So it is in my interests to keep them ill for as long as possible. Therefore, the groans of a nice lingering illness are music to my ears: the symphony of coins jingling in my pocket. And therefore a quick and painless death produces a dreadful cacophony: a hollow jangling, an awful jarring, a wicked, wasteful jiggling...
Midwife I get that sometimes.

Doctor (*greedily*) You do? One ear or two? I'm doing a special offer on eardrums at the moment.

Midwife You could be wrong.

Doctor The tragedy of my profession, madam, is that I am never wrong; its one consolation that, if I am, I always bury my mistakes.

Man I demand a recount!

Midwife (*sighing*) Oh, very well. Rewind. (*She takes the pram to* UC, *placing it next to the wheelchair and stands beside it*)

Doctor, Man and Wife rewind their positions to the beginning of the play

Doctor I'm sorry.

Wife I called you as soon as...

Doctor Your husband had a heart attack a few minutes ago. Naturally, I did all I could, but at his age...

Wife Forty-five.

Man Forty-three! Forty-three!

Doctor ...it is usually fatal. Now if he'd been older...

Man Well, give or take a year.

Wife Thank you, Doctor.

Wife and Doctor come round to the back of the sofa, she DS

Doctor I'll write you out a death certificate now for the undertaker.

Wife Sorry.

Man Stop apologising, woman!

Doctor What will you do, do you think?

Wife Well, cry, obviously. Then, I'm not sure. All this time on my hands. I might—I know it sounds silly—but I've always fancied line-dancing.

Man What?

Wife And of course there's the insurance.

Man What insurance?

Wife I could go on a cruise. It might help me to forget.

Man comes down to his Wife

Man But I don't want you to forget!

Wife Of course I'll miss him ... his funny little ways ... although I have to admit, some of them were slightly irritating, many of them boring and a few quite disgusting.

Man This is your husband you are talking about here, woman!

Wife I especially disliked his habit of calling me "woman". As if I didn't know I was a woman.

Doctor approaches her

Doctor And a very fine specimen too, if I may say so.
Wife (*coyly giggling*) Oh, thank you. (*Recovering her composure*) Sorry.
  You'll have to forgive me, I'm not used to compliments. I've been married
  for eighteen years.
Doctor But I meant—what will you do *now*, meaning in the next half hour?
Wife Oh.
Doctor Is there somewhere you could go? Friends? Neighbours?
Wife Young couple. Very nice. In the apartment next door. I don't know
  what they'll be doing right now.

*We find out. The young couple suddenly become more animated. She needs
both hands to separate out a ladle of her sticky macaroni cheese and to dump
it on to his plate. He sticks a forkful into his mouth and chews thoughtfully.
It has the consistency of chewing gum. She sits crossly*

Young Woman I wish you'd eat with your mouth closed!
Young Man I'm hungry.
Young Woman You don't need to wolf it down like you'll never be fed
  again!
Young Man I never know with you.
Young Woman What's that mean?
Young Man There you go again. Biting my head off.
Young Woman (*wiping cheese sauce off her cheek*) And there you go again,
  spitting your food all over the place!

They freeze

Wife Probably arguing. They usually do around this time. Young couples
  always start early. Have you noticed that? The older you get, the later in
  the day you start to row. Till in the end, I suppose, you're too old to care.

Wife has lightened the mood. Doctor plays along

Doctor Or remember.

Wife goes sad again

Wife I'm so sorry. I do apologise.
Doctor No, no, it is I who am sorry. My deepest...
Wife And mine.

Doctor approaches, hands over the certificate and kisses her hand. She curtsies in her embarrassment

Doctor Condolences. (*He freezes*)
Wife (*looking at the certificate*) What lovely ... handwriting. (*She sits on the back of the sofa, desolately looking out* R)

Doctor stands above her, a comforting hand on her shoulder. Man breaks RC

Man I'm too young to die!
Midwife Who else would you prefer?
Man Pardon?

Midwife takes a step DS

Midwife Someone died. Who would you prefer died in your place? One of them? (*She points at the young couple*)
Man No, they're too young.
Midwife (*pointing to Doctor*) Him?
Man Well, it's not for me—but ... yes. (*He moves* DS *to take a closer look at him*)
Doctor Excuse me. But I *am* a doctor. In fact, a consultant. If doctors were to die, who would tell the living from the dead?
Man We'd know. It's obvious.
Doctor But would you accept the obvious?
Man Yes.
Doctor All right, you're dead.
Man No!
Doctor See what I mean? At least with a doctor on call you have a dispassionate professional opinion to resolve disputes.
Man Who gives you the authority?
Doctor You do.
Man I want a second opinion.
Doctor Gladly. (*He spins round*) You're dead.
Man All right. Not doctors ... er.
Doctor (*hopefully*) Patients? I could run the most efficient Health Service without patients. Even politicians could run a *fairly* efficient Health Service without patients. No? Then how about teachers?

Young Woman suddenly springs up and protests, causing Man to spin round

Young Woman No! Pupils. Just give me one month without the children and I could get my classroom tidy. Give me two and I might even finish the marking!

Her husband coughs. Embarrassed and confused—she can't think what came over her—she picks up the plates and turns to the sink, URC

Doctor May I go now?

Midwife links arms with him and takes him DRC

Midwife There is one thing I've always wanted to know. Pardon my ignorance, but what is the difference—between a doctor and a consultant?
Doctor (*in jovial mood*) A doctor—that is, a general practitioner—knows a little about a lot. A consultant knows a lot about a little.
Midwife So the difference is less and less.
Doctor Except in terms of our fee. Which is more and more.
Midwife I'll remember that. Thank you, Doctor. (*She turns up to* C)
Old Man (*dropping out of character and speaking conspiratorially*) Er... You seem to be the one in charge here?
Old Woman (*dropping out of character*) Go on.
Old Man (*suddenly sounding like an old actor: perfect—if exaggerated—elocution and any excuse to get out of a rehearsal before the pub closes*) Will you be needing me in the next scene? Only I need to go for a quick pee.
Man I don't believe this! I am *dying* and no-one seems to care!
Old Man Correction. You are *dead* and no-one cares.

Young Man rises

Young Man Why should we? It's not happening to us. (*He turns up to the sink and starts drying the dishes*)
Old Man Please?
Old Woman Oh. Make it a quick one.

Old Man heads for the exit DR

And say one for me while you're at it.

Old Man looks puzzled, then exits DR

Man I'm not ready to die!
Old Woman Ah! Now that's a whole new kettle of kippers. Do you think *she* is?

Man takes a step towards his Wife

Man My wife?

Wife rises

I don't know. Women know more about these things.

Slowly, Wife walks to the DS arm of the sofa, oblivious to this conversation, looking at her husband's corpse on the sofa

Old Woman Oh, so you'd like her to be dead instead of you?
Man No! *(Realizing this for the first time)* I love her.
Old Woman Good. For a moment there I wasn't sure.

Wife turns away from the corpse and sits on the DS arm of sofa, facing out R

Man Nor was I. She's changed. *(Fascinated, he crosses to his wife)* When did she start to look like this? Even her voice, so hard and worn.
Old Woman How many years were you married?
Man Eighteen.
Old Woman Then at a rough guess I'd say it started...
Man *(turning away from his Wife)* Strange, I can't remember...
Old Woman What?
Man ...the colour of her eyes.

Old Woman turns away to the table RC, pulls off the tablecloth and shakes it

Old Woman Same as mine. Now, come on. You're dead. Time you were gone.
Man You look familar too. Familiar but strange.
Old Woman *(re-laying the cloth neatly)* So I should. You've seen me every day of your life. I've burped you, bathed you, dried your eyes and kissed it better. I've shouted, "You'll be late for school!" and "Last orders, please". I've mended your broken leg and your broken heart. And listened to you rabbit on about yourself and your wants and your hopes and your dreams—day after week after month after year. But now—now it's me who'll do the harping and you who'll do the listening.
Man I don't understand.

Old Woman stops and turns to him

Old Woman I was your nan, your char, your neighbour, the woman behind the counter, tea lady, dinner lady, the old lady on the bus you wouldn't stand up for, the nurse in the vaccination programme you wouldn't sit down for——
Man All right, all right. *(He kneels before his Wife)* I wish now I'd seen her, really seen her. And told her.

Old Woman Well, you can't.
Man Who'll take care of her now?
Old Woman Not you. (*She pauses slightly*) You left her provided for, didn't you? (*She slowly walks* C)
Man Well…
Old Woman You made a will?
Man I was going to.
Old Woman You told her you loved her?
Man I'm not good with words. I left it to the cards.
Old Woman Cards?
Man Oh, you know—birthday cards——

Wife finds the last card he sent, stuck down the back of the sofa. She opens it

Wife (*remembering the verse in the last one he sent*)
          Happy Birthday to my Wife
          I shall love you all my Life
          'Cos you're really Nice.

Wife and Old Woman shudder. Man falls backwards in shock, but Wife cannot see him

Man (*defensively*) And Christmas cards. And anniversary——
Old Woman When you remembered.
Man Well, it was a difficult date to remember.
Old Woman ⎤
              ⎟ (*together*) Humpf!
Wife   ⎦

Man scrambles to his feet and moves towards Old Woman

Man And presents. I bought her presents. The love was in the presents.
Wife A dressing-gown. Pink. Candlewick. (*She throws the birthday card away in disgust*)
Man And a pair of fluffy slippers.
Old Woman Says it all. (*She returns to the pram* UC)

Man follows her

Man What will happen now?

Wife crosses despondently to her neighbour's flat, suddenly alone, suddenly vulnerable. She knocks on their door. Young Woman answers. Sensing her distress, Young Woman hugs her

Old Woman Perhaps her neighbours will take care of her. Or perhaps she'll take your advice.
Man I don't remember giving her any.

Wife sits US *of their table and is comforted by the Young Woman. The Young Man,* URC, *makes them mugs of coffee*

Wife The only advice I ever remember him giving anyone was "There's plenty more fish in the sea".
Young Woman (*looking coldly at her own husband*) Now where have I heard that before?
Man That was for men not for women!
Young Woman What will you do? With all that time on your hands?
Wife I'll get a decent night's sleep for once.
Young Woman (*with feeling*) Ooh yes! (*She glares at her husband*)

Young Man brings the coffee to the table

Wife And I thought … line-dancing.
Young Woman (*eagerly*) Can I come too?
Wife But the washing-up?
Young Woman (*dismissively, to her husband*) He'll do that.
Wife I really ought to finish the ironing——
Young Man But——
Young Woman He'll do that.

Young Man is taken aback, but quickly relents

Young Man Yeah, OK.
Man (*horrified*) Stop!

They freeze. Man comes C

All right. I made a mess of it. Got it wrong.
Old Woman And now you'll have plenty of time to work out how.
Man I wish I had it over. My life.

Old Woman saunters C, *enjoying this*

Old Woman They all say that.
Man If only I knew then what I know now.
Old Woman You did. You just didn't listen.
Man No, I mean it. If I could go back, work out where I went wrong, put it right. Nana? Please? (*He takes Old Woman's arm, like a nagging child*)

Old Woman Oh no, absolutely no. No, no, not for a minute, no.
Man Pretty please?
Old Woman If I gave you twenty minutes where would it end?
Man Twenty!
Old Woman All right, twenty-five. But not a minute more.
Man Oh, nana, I love you the bestest! (*He dances, spinning Old Woman*)
Old Woman Put me down! Thirty minutes tops. Now. Where do you want
to start? How about we go back and visit you as a child?
Man Oh, little innocent me!
Old Woman That's not the child *I* remember.
Man All right.
Old Woman Selfish, manipulative, obstinate, self-willed. I know. I was his
nana.

*Woman rises, changing accent and posture as she changes character from
Wife to Mother*

Man All right.
Mother And the temper on him. I know. I was his mother.
Man (*having a tantrum*) All right, all right, all right! Not as a child!
Old Woman You'll have to in the end, you know—we all do—in the end
we all meet ourselves coming back. Oh, well. How about him? (*She points
to Young Man*) Sweet sixteen? All urges and surges.
Man Yes!

Young Man slouches and grumbles into his role as Teenager

Old Woman Rather you than me. What do we need? Mother?
Mother Here.
Old Woman Sister?

*Young Woman rises, changing accent and posture as she changes character
from Neighbour to seventeen-year-old Sister*

Sister Here.

*They cross to the sofa, angle it to face DL, then sit down to watch TV, Mother
DS. Teenager remains in the kitchen and sits R of the table. He gets out his
homework*

Man (*nervously*) Can he hear me?
Old Woman Yes.
Man Can he see me?
Old Woman No.

Man Right. I'll talk to him. Put him right.
Old Woman Word of warning. He might not listen.
Man Of course he'll listen! It's *me* talking. To *myself.* I'm bound to listen to *me.* It stands to reason.
Old Woman (*unimpressed*) Ah, reason. I'll get on with the washing-up then.

Lights on cyc change to a bloodier hue. We are now in the kitchen on a typical sixteen year-old's midweek evening. Old Woman, as Nana, is washing the dishes, URC. *Teenager is trying to do his homework while his Mother and older Sister are watching TV in the other room, the Sister flipping through a magazine in a bored sort of way*

Teenager (*bellowing*) Will you two shut up in there!
Man Us?
Old Woman No. Them.

Man starts to walk into the kitchen, RC, *seeing the room again as it was thirty years ago*

Man I remember.
Teenager (*shouting*) Will you turn that telly down? I can't hear myself think in here!
Mother What does he want now?
Sister (*shrugging*) I don't know.
Mother Find out what your brother wants.
Sister (*shouting over the back of the sofa*) What do you want?
Teenager (*shouting back*) I can't hear you over the telly.
Sister (*shouting even louder*) I can't hear you over the telly.
Mother Tell him to speak up. He's always mumbling these days.
Sister (*pointing at TV*) Oh look! It's whatsit!
Teenager They don't understand...

Man stands at the US *end of the table and leans forward*

Man I do.
Teenager ...what it's like.
Man I do.
Teenager Oh, what's the point!

Man sits US *of the table*

Man The point is this. You're special. Unique. There's no-one like you in all the world. Never has been. Never will be.
Teenager I don't know what to do!

Man Find your gift. Each of us has one special gift—a wonderful mixture of talent, insights, experience and——
Teenager (*exasperated*) Oh!
Man —temperament—that makes us unique. That's your gift to the world. Life's gift to you. And your job in life is to find that gift. Explore, cherish and share your gift with the world. (*He stands up and addresses Old Woman*) That's not bad. In fact, it's very good. And more than that, it's true. It's very true.
Old Woman So what went wrong?
Man All right. You try.
Old Woman I did.
Man Try again.
Old Woman (*sighing, handing him a tea towel*) Dry these. (*She stands beside Teenager, her hands on his shoulders*)
Teenager They don't understand. What I'm going through.
Nana We've all been there...
Teenager No-one understands.
Nana ...we just all of us forget.
Teenager Sometimes I just want to give up. School, home. Pack it in. Run away. Then they'll be sorry.
Nana Yes. And so will you. (*She crosses to stand* DS *of him*)

Teenager rises

Teenager Why can't they see? The world is a mess. But it's like only I can see it. They've given up. They just shrug their shoulders and keep their heads down and pretend it will all go away or somehow right itself. But it won't. I know that. And I know how to make it right. I can change things and make the world a better place. I can do it. I know I can. They're too old. But I've got the time. They're too lazy. But I've got the energy. They've had their chance. Now it's my turn. I can do it—do it all—which is why it's so unfair! (*He sits*)
Nana What is?
Teenager That first I have to get GCE maths! I mean, what does maths matter? It's the meaning of life I'm dealing with here! Why maths? Why me?

Man comes to the US *side of Teenager*

Man Stick at it. With maths you can go to University. Get a good job.
Nana Then you can forget all about maths.

Man is looking over the boy's shoulder

Teenager It's not fair! (*He fills in another answer*) Sixty-seven.
Man (*correcting the sum*) Seventy-six.
Teenager I'll show them.
Nana Of course you will. (*She takes the drying cloth and moves* URC, *to stir soup on the stove*)
Man Not with sixty-seven he won't.
Teenager I'll be rich and famous. Then they'll be sorry.
Man Yes. No.

Teenager rises

Teenager Oh no! It's happening again. I'm sweating. Do you know the first thing I'll do? When I know everything? I'll invent a cure for puberty. (*He breaks* DR) No more flushes and blushes and gallons of sweat and stink and ... things. I'll be able to say, "You are my body and you are under my control. You are my brain and you will think what I tell you, when I tell you, and *you will never embarrass me on public transport again!*" (*He begins to break to* DC) And when someone says—oh, something clever and cutting—I'll be able to come back with just the right words. Kapow! And I'll be smooth and cool and ... and not sweaty and sticky and covered in zits!
Man I'd forgotten. (*He sinks in to the chair* R *of the table*)

Teenager crosses up to RC

Teenager Do you know my greatest fear? That one day someone will squeeze me—and I'm so oily and sweaty and sticky—I'll just go *pfit* and pop out of my shirt—my whole body will pop out of my clothes and up in the air and I'll be up there in full view of everyone—stark bollock naked— and they'll all laugh! Because they don't understand. No-one understands ... what it's like ... to be me!

Nana crosses to him

Nana Give me a hug.
Teenager No! Nana! I'll squither out like a tube of jelly!
Nana I like jelly.
Teenager I'll squirt and splodge, just one great greasy splat on the floor.
Nana Then I'll wipe you up and cuddle you 'cos I love you.
Teenager Oh Nana! (*He breaks to the* US *end of the table, facing* US)

Man rises

Man You know his trouble?

Old Woman He's sixteen.
Man He won't listen.
Old Woman This is *you* we're talking about.
Man He's so bound up in himself, so full of himself——

Teenager turns on an imaginary character sitting US *of the table*

Teenager You can talk.
Man What?
Old Woman Ah yes. The catch. Sorry. I tried to explain.

Old Woman crosses RC, *tasting the soup on the stove and adding a pinch more salt, while the Teenager points a finger at his imaginary opponent*

Teenager You sit there, smugly dealing out advice.
Man He can't see me?
Old Woman Oh no.
Man He doesn't know that one day he'll end up as me?
Old Woman Gracious no. The shock would kill him. (*She adds some salt, then puts the lid back on the saucepan and turns the heat down*)

Teenager turns on another imaginary opponent, sitting DS *of the table, narrowly missing accusing the audience directly*

Teenager Did you follow your own advice? When you were my age?
Man Cheeky kid.
Old Woman You see, he knew a lot of grown-ups, just like you. (*She begins to return to her dishes* UR)
Man How could I follow my own advice? I hadn't heard it.
Old Woman You did. (*She points to the seats round the table, real and imaginary*) Uncles. Teachers. Friends of the family. You know how it is. Like pass the parcel. Everyone wants to give advice. No-one wants to take it.

Man sits R *of the table*

Man He could at least pay attention—listen.
Old Woman Did you?

Teenager walks round the table to face Man. He leans over the table

Teenager You tell me you had ideals. Where are they now? You were going to make a difference—to make the world a better place. Is it? Well?
Old Woman Well?

Man rises and leans over the table to face Teenager

Man You'll get a clip round the ear, my lad.
Teenager You don't know nothing!
Man Grammar! "You don't know *anything*."

Old Woman comes forward to the US end of the table

Old Woman And that's how all advice ends up—with a clip round the ear
and a lesson in grammar.

*Man crosses US of the table to Old Woman. At the same time, Teenager
crosses to the DS end of the table. This should give the effect of them
shadowing each other*

Man There's no speaking to young people these days. Why, in *my* day——
Old Woman And which days were these, then?

*Man breaks to the oven RC and pulls off the pan lid angrily. At the same time,
Teenager crosses to the chair R of the table and angrily opens his maths book*

Man Oh, get on with your homework!

Teenager sits

      And another thing!
Old Woman ⎱ (*together*) What?
Teenager ⎰
Man There is far too much salt in this soup!
Old Woman Right. Had enough? Ready to move on?

Man crosses to the kitchen door UC to yell at his family in the lounge

Man (*bellowing*) Will you turn that telly down? I can't hear myself think in
here!

Mother rises angrily and moves toward the kitchen

Sister Did you hear that? (*Vindictively*) Go on, mum. Get him!
Old Woman Definitely time to move on.
Man I'd forgotten. How angry I was. How confused and afraid and angry.
All the time. Lord, how I hated being a teenager! Just one endless round
of arguments and rows and——

Mother enters the kitchen

Mother How dare you speak to me like that!

Teenager rises

Teenager I didn't say anything.
Mother Go to your room!
Teenager I'm going!

Teenager exits UR

Mother Oh, I'm sorry, Mrs Muggins. (*She turns away to the oven*)
Man Pardon?
Old Woman She means me. (*With a Northern accent, not too pronounced*)
Oh, don't worry, dear. Being a cleaner you see in everyone's nooks and
crannies.

Mother tests the soup

Man You do?
Cleaner I went looking under your mattress once. Never again.

Cleaner breaks to R *of the table*

Mother (*absent-mindedly*) Not enough salt. (*She adds two generous pinches
of salt, then sweeps past Man and sits above the table*)
Cleaner (*to Mother*) Kids are the same everywhere. You can't go blaming
yourself.
Mother But I do.
Cleaner How about a nice cup of tea? (*She pours it*)
Mother Oh Mrs Muggins, you wouldn't believe how hard it is to love your
own children sometimes.

Man stands between them, leaning over the table

Man Excuse me. This is supposed to be *my* story.
Cleaner Which is part of *her* story which is part of——
Man All right.
Cleaner So shut up and listen—you might learn something. (*To Mother*) Go
on, dear.
Mother They grow up too fast.
Cleaner They do.

Mother Before you know it, they're so big and bolshie—and blundering about. Always breaking things...

Man Oh, she's not still on about that porcelain figurine! (*He breaks to* R *of the table*)

Mother Family heirloom, that was.

Cleaner I'll have a go with the Bostik later.

Mother He's breaking my heart. Clumsy great oaf. I'm afraid he'll hurt himself, and other people, and be hurt, and unhappy, and I won't be there to...

Cleaner There, there. Blow on this. (*She clicks her fingers urgently*)

Man looks round, grabs the tea towel, passes it to her. She passes it to Mother

Mother You want to keep them young and safe and locked away somewhere. (*She blows noisily into the towel, then hands it back*) Sorry. I do love him. I just can't find the words any more. When I do, when I try, he pulls away, as if, as if he hates me.

Cleaner hands the tea towel to Man, who looks round then puts it in the washing basket DR. *Cleaner tops up the tea in the mugs*

Cleaner And you hate that...

Mother It hurts.

Cleaner So you hurt back.

Mother He's got such a temper on him.

Cleaner Your temper.

Mother He thinks he knows best.

Cleaner And you know better.

Mother He's too young.

Cleaner And you're getting no younger.

Pause while they both sip their tea

Mother Too much sugar. (*She puts down her mug*) I've only to say one thing——

Cleaner And he does another.

Mother These days I just have to see him to go *Aargh*!

Cleaner You want to smother him with kisses.

Mother But I can't.

Cleaner So instead you want to...

Mother Strangle him! What's wrong with me, Mrs Muggins?

Cleaner rises and collects their mugs

Cleaner You're the mother of a teenage son, love. And there's no cure but time.
Man And time, might I remind you, Nana Muggins, has almost run out.

Man follows Old Woman to the sink URC

Old Woman (*resuming her own accent*) I've told you before. Your story is part of her story and her story is part of our story and our story is part of The Story and——
Man Point taken!
Old Woman Good!

Old Man enters DR

Mother sees him. She rises and rushes to him. They meet DRC, *below the table. She throws her arms round his neck. Through the following dialogue, Old Woman takes a new tea towel from the drawer. She hands it to Man. Old Woman rinses the mugs and hands them to him to dry*

Mother Oh Dad!
Old Man There, there.
Mother Dad? Why are boys so difficult?
Old Man My dearest daughter. Just be grateful you never had two girls!

Old Woman comes DC, *drying her hands*

Old Woman All change. Where next?

The Lights on the cyc change. No colour this time, just a bare, uncompromising light. It is as if the performance has stopped and the rehearsal lights have been switched back on

For the first time we see everyone except Man as the people they really are— actors, stepping in and out of role as the script demands. And we see their real personalities

Old Woman is the perfect Stage Manager: totally in charge, totally unflappable. Even now she is flipping through an invisible prompt copy to check what is needed for the next scene and marking a few notes with a pencil drawn from behind her right ear

Old Man, now leaning against the desk and tying his shoelace, is a bombastic old has-been who loves the sound of his own voice, and is trying to cope with the fact that he is becoming more than a little forgetful. He knows, but he will not let himself admit, that this could be his last season in the company

Young Man is in his first season as Juvenile Lead, so he knows all the world adores him and can perfectly understand why

No wonder, then, that Woman is cynically impervious to men's charms and ready to console any poor actress foolish enough to be taken in by those wolves. Even as she walks over to the sofa, takes off her shoes and rubs her feet, she is impressive: strong and versatile, as a woman and an actress

Young Woman, rising and stretching now, is still too new at this game. An amateur in her first professional engagement, she is too easily over-awed by everything and everyone, but she is a fast learner

Only Man is still enthusiastically involved in the action, but then, it is his life they are acting out, and like a gifted but inexperienced author attending the rehearsals of the first professional production of one of his plays, he still believes he matters. Oh, foolish man! And like all writers, he blithers on regardless

Man My first job.
Woman (*to Old Woman*) Do you mind if I sit this one out? I'm totally drained.
Young Woman It's all that raw emotion.
Woman No, it's these new shoes.
Young Woman I could do with a bit of raw emotion.
Woman Oh, your chance will come, dear.
Young Woman I mean—that last scene—Big Sister—hardly Juliet, was it?

Old Woman takes a step RC

Old Woman Where's Jimmy*? (**Substitute Young Man's real name*)
Old Man Oh, I don't know. Take my last line—rather affecting, I thought.
Woman (*darkly*) Very.

Man comes DC

Man My first job. My first pay packet. The feeling that at last I was beginning to be noticed.
Old Woman (*in a conciliatory tone*) You were wonderful, Jack*. (**Substitute Old Man's real name*) You always are. Jimmy*!
Old Man Thank you, my dear. Nice to be appreciated.
Man (*strongly*) I said, "I was beginning to be noticed."

Young Man enters UR *and moves* R *of the table*

Young Man Sorry. I just——
Woman } (*without even looking round; together*) Zip!
Young Woman

Young Man does up his flies

Young Man Sorry.
Young Woman Honestly. What is it about men and their bladders?

Old Man walks round the back of the table, moving US *as he speaks*

Old Man Golden rule of the theatre, sonny. Never talk on an upstage move and never ... whatever.
Old Woman Are we all here now? Good. (*To Man*) Sorry, dear. You were saying?
Man My first step on the ladder of life!

Old Man brings Young Man to the back of the chair R *of the table, his left arm round Young Man's shoulder*

Old Man I remember my first step. Manchester* it was. The old Lyceum*. (**Adapt to local theatre history*) Gone now. Everything is. That's where I learnt the Golden Rule of Theatre. (*He uses his left hand, apparently, to clean out Young Man's ear*) Never make distracting hand gestures, and never, ever... (*But he still can't remember the rule*)
Man My first chance to make a difference.
Old Man (*at last he remembers*) ...wear zips!

Everyone double-takes. Man makes a despairing gesture and crosses to the US *arm of the sofa, where he will sit and watch the action over the back of the sofa. Old Woman shrugs and orders the cast into their positions*

Old Woman Manager: forceful, dynamic...
Old Man Ah! Me again! (*He sits* R *of the table, unrolls his newspaper, begins to read. Typically, he has not bothered to read the stage directions and plays the Manager as hearty, unthinking, uncaring ... and more than a little venial*)
Old Woman ...over the hill.
Woman (*muttering*) And over the top.
Old Woman Our hero? Aged twenty-two.
Young Man It's typecasting, it really is! (*He takes the* US *chair and places*

it facing the Old Man's chair, then leaves the "office" by miming opening and closing a door RC)

Old Woman And two assorted clerks: female.

Young Woman Typical. (*She stomps* UC, *collects the bench and brings it* DC)

Woman (*to Old Woman*) Would you mind?

Old Woman Oh, very well.

Woman takes no further interest in the scene. She puts her feet up, facing US. *Old Woman helps Young Woman position the bench* DC

(*To Young Woman*) Actually, I don't mind at all. I like the company.

Young Woman I like the pay. (*She sits on one end of the bench, facing off* R, *and starts filling in forms, which she puts in a tray* DC)

Old Clerk, sitting on the other end, facing off L, *takes forms from the tray, glances briefly at them, then files them. They will continue this throughout the office scene. They are never idle. When business is slow, Young Clerk files her nails and Old Clerk knits. Their actions should have a flow and monotony which suggest years of practice*

Manager turns a page in his newspaper, finds the crossword, reaches out for a biro without even needing to look up for it, and starts to fill the crossword in

Young Man adjusts his tie and knocks on the office door. Manager smoothly opens a large file, hides his paper and closes the file. Again, years of practice are suggested. Young Man enters the office. Manager rises

Manager Congratulations, my boy. Executive Officer, eh? How does it feel?

Young Man sits

Young Man Wonderful. Really, it's——

Manager Good, good.

Young Man —so wonderful to be earning my own keep——

Manager crosses above the table to Young Man

Manager You'll start out here.

Young Man I just want to start at the bottom and—— (*He rises*)

Manager brings him toward C

Manager And what very attractive bottoms they are.

Young Man ⎫
Old Clerk ⎬ (*together*) Eh?
Young Clerk ⎭
Manager Sorry.
Old Clerk No improvisation.
Young Man Just think. My own master!

Manager brings Young Man to the outer office, DC

Manager Answering to me as Senior Executive Officer...
Young Man Able to choose when I work...
Manager Hours and conditions as laid down in contract of employment...
Young Man No more nine-to-four school days...
Manager Nine-to-five, of course, now.
Young Man Oh. Of course.
Manager These are your subordinates.
Young Man You mean, I'm over them?
Manager Well, try not to be *all* over them. Save that for coffee breaks, lunch breaks, tea breaks and the Civil Service Inter-Departmental Mixed Sauna on a Tuesday evening.
Young Man I can't wait.
Manager Bring your own towel.
Young Man Eh?
Manager Keen?
Young Man Eager.
Manager Strange ... for a moment ... a glint in your eye, tone in your voice ... like looking in a mirror. I can see I shall have to watch you, my boy. Well, enjoy! (*He returns to his office and his newspaper, firmly shutting the door behind him*)
Young Man Good morning. I'm——
Old Clerk —the new Exec. Well, I'm the Senior Clerical and she's the Junior Clerical.
Young Man Hi. What, er, do I do—exactly?
Old Clerk Exactly, this. (*She rises and gives him a lightning tour of the outer office*)

Indeed, the rest of the scene should go at such speed and yet clarity that it earns you a round of applause!

Files alphabetical: A to Z before you, Overflow and Outsize behind you, Dead to your right, Pending to your left. Here: forms, numerical. She fills in a form for each new applicant, hands it to you for checking, then to me for filing, alpha——
Young Man —betically. I get the picture. And that's it?

Young Clerk Thirty-nine hours a week.
Young Man (*incredulously*) For that we get paid?

Old Clerk resumes her seat and the familiar work pattern begins. Start slow,
then build up speed

Old Clerk Earns you gross salary...
Young Clerk Forty-six weeks a year.
Old Clerk Plus annual increments...
Young Clerk Forty years of your life.
Old Clerk Minus National Insurance, Pension Contributions, Income Tax,
   Sundries.
Young Clerk To the top of the incremental ladder.
Young Man Then?
Young Clerk Promotion.
Old Clerk From Clerical Officer.
Young Clerk Us.
Old Clerk To Executive Officer.
Young Clerk You.
Old Clerk To Senior Executive Officer.
Young Clerk Him.
Young Man (*wide-eyed and hopeful*) Then?
Young Clerk Pension.

The work has dried up so Young Clerk reverts to the care of her cuticles and
Old Clerk to her knitting

Old Clerk At x eightieths of final salary to a maximum of forty eightieths,
   averaged over last three years of working life.
Young Clerk Making room for one more new recruit at Clerical...
Old Clerk Or Executive...
Young Clerk ...level. Get it?
Young Man Got it.
Old Clerk Good.
Young Man Where do we start?
Young Clerk Tea break.

Young Woman exits UL

Old Woman goes to the back of the sofa. Young Man spins round, trying to
catch one of them, but they are too fast for him. Dejected and exhausted, he
sits on the bench, facing UC

Old Woman I'm jiggered.

Woman Now you know why I wanted this scene off.

Manager comes out of his office

Manager Getting the hang of it, are we?
Young Man Just one thing I don't understand.
Manager Ask away. After all, what are the fruits of experience for ... if not ... whatever?
Young Man Why?

Man rises and comes to his right shoulder

Man You had ideals.
Manager Why? (*He comes to his left shoulder*)
Man You were going to make a difference.
Young Man Why?

Manager and Man swap places

Man To make the world a better place.
Manager Why? Because, my boy, in the words of the immortal Bard, it pays your bloody wages!

Man breaks up to the table. Manager sighs, then tries again

(*Trying to be patient*) We all have our reason for doing this job—any job. Security. Ambition. (*Exasperated*) Because it helps to pass the time. (*Calming down again*) Take Doris here. (*He goes and fetches Old Clerk*)
Old Clerk Dora.

Man turns and leans against the desk, watching this

Manager Been with us, man and boy, twenty-six years——
Old Clerk Twenty-seven in October.

Young Man rises

Young Man And you're still sane?
Manager Not a question we ever ask, dear boy. You just keep on doing it and who knows, in five—ten years—if you're lucky—there might be a vacancy—promotion, even—Aberkenny, Doncaster—always a vacancy in London. So, chop chop, blink blink, what what? (*He turns* US *and enters his office, calling out as he does so*) Shirley!

Young Clerk enters UL

Young Clerk (*correcting him, crossly*) Sarah!
Manager Whatever. (*He returns to his office*)

Old Clerk and Young Clerk resume their places on the bench, Young Man standing behind the bench, between them

Young Clerk (*with a sigh, filling in a form*) Chop chop. (*She passes the form to Young Man*)

He checks it, cursorily

Young Man Blink blink.
Old Clerk (*filing it*) What what.

This is repeated several times, getting faster but more careless, then grinding down to slower and almost zombie-like as the "working day" wears on. During this, Man turns and walks slowly DR, *the memory too painful for him. Manager makes the noise of a clock chiming the hour. Suddenly they all brighten up*

Manager Five o'clock!

The two women go for their coats, UC. *Young Man helps Old Clerk on with her coat. They stand* LC

Old Clerk You'll get used to it.
Young Man How?
Old Clerk Personally, I look at the alternative. Which in my case means living with my sister in Herne Bay.

He looks puzzled, so she tries to explain in a very matter of fact way

I never married so I have to support myself. And that's fine by me. There's nothing I'd rather be doing with my time, so I don't care if my job does take it up 'cos it was no good to me anyway. I have no special skills, no advanced education, so I feel I'm lucky to have got this job. Even this job. For me, it means independence, freedom. Getting away from parents who ignored me and a sister who looked down on me, and into a little bedsit in a small town far, far away. Then of getting away from my little bedsit and neighbours who ignore me and married friends who look down on me, and into a little office in a small department far, far away. Where I sit, from nine to five, ignored by my inferiors and looked down on by my superiors, filing dockets on people we can all safely ignore and look down on because they're even more unemployable and disabled than we are.

Young Man I'm sorry. I never...

Old Clerk ...listened? Or cared?

Young Man I'm sorry.

Old Clerk crosses DC *to the bench to collect her handbag*

Old Clerk So you should be. I've only one dread, retirement; only one fear, redundancy—'cos on x eightieths of what I earn, I won't be able to afford to go on living in my little bedsit off the High Street, all alone except for changing my library books Tuesday and Choir Practice Thursday. I'll have to move in with my sister, who was a teacher and is a bully and lives in Herne Bay. She'll resent it, of course, so she'll bully me. That's what I have to look forward to, young man: being bullied into early retirement then bullied into an early grave. Which is why I thank God on my knees every night for every weary, lonely, futile day of my working life. Good night, young man.

Old Man looks up, concerned. Woman rises, suddenly, deeply moved. Old Woman goes to her. They sit on the sofa together, comforting each other. Old Man goes back to his crossword, turning his chair to face US

Young Man I think I upset her.

Young Clerk comes to RC

Young Clerk Funny—people like her—you don't think of them having feelings.

Young Man Would you, er, like to go for a drink?

Young Clerk Yes.

Young Man I mean, I know you're busy.

Young Clerk I'm not.

Young Man Washing your hair or something.

Young Clerk Well, I could if you want.

Young Man Not that you look like the sort of woman who spends her evenings washing her hair.

Young Clerk What?

Young Man What?

Man And so it happened. My first date. (*He moves the slatted bench* DLC, *facing out* L, *then stands above the sofa, to watch*)

Woman and Old Woman angle the sofa to face the bench so they have a

ringside seat. Young Man and Young Clerk make their way slowly in an arc from RC *towards it*

Young Man I'm going to make it, Shirley.
Young Clerk (*correcting him*) Sarah.
Young Man Right to the top.
Young Clerk That bus is a long time coming. (*She sits forlornly on the bench, facing out* L. *It is getting cold. She shivers*)
Man Why?
Young Man So everyone can see that I've made it. That I'm somebody.
Young Clerk Yes, John.

He jumps up on to the bench

Young Man Someone to notice, to look up to.

She looks up at him

Young Clerk (*miserably*) I want to go home.
Young Man OK. (*He jumps down*) Your place or mine?

Young Clerk rises in tears and walks away, DC

Hang on, I bought you dinner!

Young Clerk turns on him, furious now

Young Clerk You ... unspeakable...
Woman Speak it, dear!
Young Clerk ...unutterable...
Old Woman Utter it, utter it!

Young Man turns away and combs his hair in a shop window

Young Man (*to his image*) Who loves ya, baby?
Woman
Old Woman } (*together*) You do!
Old Man

Young Clerk arches above and behind him to C

Young Clerk Self, self, self! You want everyone to see it your way? Then start by seeing it his way, her way, our way. You're special? So are they.

Unique? So are we. Fragile? So am I. (*She crosses to the* DS *end of the table, sobbing*)
Young Man But your bus——
Man (*amazed*) What did she say?
Woman
Old Woman | (*together*) Self, self, self!
Old Man
Man I don't remember any of this!

Young Man has turned his back to the audience, facing UR. *He crosses his hands over his chest and then starts fondling his waist, shoulders and hair, giving the audience the impression he is locked in a passionate embrace*

Young Man (*totally lost in self-love*) Gimme a kiss, you gorgeous hunk, you!
Man I remember that.
Young Man (*getting more and more excited*) Oh! Oh! Oh!
Young Clerk Self, self, self!
Man Steady on!

Young Man turns to face the audience, all passion spent, a silly smirk on his face. He mimes lighting a cigarette

Young Man How was it for you?

Everyone looks accusingly at Man. He tries to defend himself

Man It was my first time!

Old Man rises

Old Man We've all tried that line, dear boy.

Young Man makes the sound of the phone ringing and sits on the bench. Manager picks up the phone in his office

Man It was ... puppy love.
Old Woman And you were the puppy.

She rises and returns to the outer office, dragging the bench back DC, *with the help of Young Man*

Young Man Shirley! (*He crosses to her*)

Young Clerk crosses back to the outer office, leaving him, in effect, facing Manager

Young Clerk Sarah! (*She turns away to her work*)

Manager puts down the phone

Manager Word in your ear, dear boy. Head Office on the line. We need to save time, save money. Any ideas?

Young Man slumps back to his work station, DC, *in the outer office, behind the two clerks*

Young Clerk (*to Old Clerk*) I hate this job. Chop, chop. A computer could do it in half the time.
Young Man Blink, blink.
Old Clerk A trained monkey could do it in half the time. But that's not the point, is it, dear? What, what.
Young Man Halve the time, halve the work, halve the staff! Eureka!

Young Clerk and Old Clerk look at him oddly, but continue working

Young Clerk Chop, chop.
Old Clerk What, what.

Young Man goes into the inner office. Action in the outer office freezes

Young Man I've got it!
Manager You have?
Young Man Computerization. One clerical officer—junior grade—can fill in each form directly on to the computer. The computer will check it. Halve the time, halve the staff.
Manager Brilliant. Promotion. All round. (*He dials HQ*) Send in Doris.

Action resumes in outer office

Old Clerk We've got a backlog here. I can't "What, what" till you've "Blink, blinked".
Young Man Manager wants you.
Old Clerk Me?

Old Clerk goes into the office as Manager puts down the phone

Young Clerk (*looking at Young Man bitterly*) Chop, chop.

Young Man Sarah?
Young Clerk Chop, chop.

Young Man sits on the bench beside her

Young Man About last night. Blink, blink.
Young Clerk Chop, chop.
Young Man I just wanted to say——

Old Clerk and Manager come out of the office. Manager helps Old Clerk into her coat

Young Clerk What's happened? Chop, chop.
Manager Well done, young man. HQ agreed. Halve the work, halve the work force.

Old Clerk comes forward

Young Man What do you mean? Blink, blink.
Old Clerk (*filing her last card*) Redundancy. Herne Bay, here I come. What, what.
Manager Give me a hand with this, would you, Doris?

Old Clerk helps Manager into his coat

Young Man But why are you…?
Manager Halve the work force, halve the management. Early retirement.

He walks UC *with Old Clerk*

Herne Bay, you say. Has it got a golf course?

Young Man rises

Young Man But what about me?
Manager Oh, don't worry. You got your promotion.

Manager and Old Clerk turn UC, *arm in arm, and freeze. Young Clerk glares at Young Man*

Young Man Sarah.

But she is far too busy to hear him. She is trying to do everybody's job at once on the new computer, and only just succeeding

Young Clerk (*quickly*) Chop, chop. Blink, blink. What, what. (*Repeat as necessary*)

Young Man goes into the office and sits behind what is now "his" desk

Man (*rising*) And then, I got married.
Young Clerk (*firmly*) Not to me, he didn't!

Lights on cyc change to that warm yellow with which the play began. Young Woman crosses UC. *Old Woman fusses with the baby in the pram. Man crosses nervously to Woman*

Man Right, well, I think we can skip the next bit. Fast forward over the married bliss, eh? Someone?

Woman rises, glares at Man, and starts to turn the sofa to face out front. Man places the bench DLC. *Young Woman helps Old Man into the wheelchair*

Old Man (*to Young Woman*) Well done, my dear. Real fire.
Young Woman Do you really think so?
Old Man I can see I shall have to keep an eye on you.
Young Woman It's just a hobby, really. Acting. I was a teacher in real life.
Old Man Real life?
Young Woman As opposed to stage life.
Old Man There's a difference?
Young Woman (*covering her confusion*) Between us? Oh, yes. You've got such … technique.
Old Man Over-rated. Passion, truth, that's what really matters.
Young Woman And talent.
Old Man I wouldn't go that far. (*He turns his wheelchair to face* US)

Old Woman stands beside her pram. They are two old people left out to dry in a municipal park. Man, feeling himself in the way, goes to the US *end of the table*

Man (*really nervous now*) No need to dwell on marriage, and so on.

Young Woman comes behind the sofa

Young Woman (*to Woman*) Why did you do it? (*She comes to the audience's* L *of the sofa*)

Woman moves to the audience's R *of the sofa. She assumes the role of Wife*

*with a wonderful smile, a determination to see the best in everyone and
however many times life knocks her down, however often she is hurt and
disappointed by the man in her life, she will always come back smiling. She
takes the cover from the back of the sofa and unfolds it*

Wife (*to Young Woman*) Give me a hand with this, will you?

Man crosses C, very nervous indeed

Man (*very nervous*) No problems there.

*Young Man is taking an interest in what Wife is saying. He rises, comes below
his desk and starts to walk up to C*

Wife You know, we were married eighteen years. And I don't think he ever
realized it. Ever cottoned on to what being married is all about.

Man intercepts Young Man

Man Girls' talk. You know how they go on.
Wife He had this crazy idea.

Man puts an arm round Young Man's shoulder and walks him RC

Man You see, marriage—true marriage—is like a boat—well, two boats—
tied alongside. That's what you do when you marry someone—you agree
to tie up alongside. Now, occasionally, of course, you pop into her boat for
a bit of the old how's-your-father—and occasionally—stormy weather,
etcetera—she can pop into your boat for a bit of the old comfort and calm—
but the rest of the time, you're still two people—two separate people—in
two separate boats. Together, but apart.

*Old Woman turns her pram to face them. Meanwhile Wife and Young Woman
spread the cover over the sofa and the bench to form a bed*

Old Woman And that's your idea of marriage, is it?
Man Yes. I read it in a book. By some bloke or——
Old Woman Ah yes. Books by blokes.
Man A very clever bloke.
Old Woman I suppose he told you that too?
Man No, it was on the cover. His publisher wrote that.
Old Woman Another bloke, I suppose?
Man Well, yes, actually.

Old Woman Blokes who write books for blokes to sell and blokes to buy.
Man (*trying to laugh it off*) What makes the world go round!
Old Woman Does it, now? (*She turns Old Man's wheelchair to face the action*)
Wife I disagree.
Man (*getting irritated*) Typical.

Young Man, intrigued, crosses to the sofa

Wife I'm not a boat. Not half a life because I'm half a couple. Not half a life because I've given half away. Not half a life because I'm half a person. But having two lives now—two lives combined, intertwined—growing—not from the weakness of being halved, but from the strength of being two in one. That's how I see it. Sorry.
Man (*to Young Man*) There? You see? Always apologising! Always wrong and always apologising! (*He storms over to the sofa and gets into the* R *side of the bed*)

Wife gets into the L *side of the bed. Man and Wife sit up in bed, pulling the bed cover up to their chests, speaking at first to the Young Man and Young Woman, who stand watching the proceedings from* R *and* L *ends of the sofa respectively*

Wife We had a row. Our first row.
Man Our first night together, right? In her flat.
Wife (*correcting him*) Apartment. He'd forgotten to renew the lease on his, so he had nowhere else to stay. I invited him to share mine. Mistake.
Man Big mistake.

They glare at each other then turn over and lie back to back

Can't sleep. Got to be up early in the morning. I'm the manager now. I can't afford to ring in sick. Got to set an example. At work. At home. But does she care?

Young Man and Young Woman, with a glance at each other, move closer and sit on the respective arms of the sofa

Wife I feel so hurt, so confused...
Man So angry, so furiously angry.
Wife ...that this place I've loved...
Man I hate this place.
Wife ...that has been my home for years——

Man Nowhere to call my own.
Wife —all mine. All I have——
Man All hers. Not mine.
Wife —I want to share it with him, but——
Man It's not mine.
Wife Ours.

Pause. They turn over and face each other

Man Perhaps we could...
Wife Buy you a desk...
Man Move things round...
Wife Turn the spare room into a sort of...
Man Study... I've always wanted a study.
Wife Then see about buying somewhere else.
Man But this place is so convenient. For work.
Wife For weekends.
Man Somewhere we can call...
Wife Home.
Man Ours. (*Pause*) Actually, I quite like this flat.
Wife (*correcting him*) Apartment. But it's very small.
Man Cheap to run. And very...

Young Man makes the sound of an alarm clock. Man gets up and goes to work, the table RC *serving as his office. He becomes Manager for the next scene. Wife luxuriates in bed*

Wife And we stayed. Married. For eighteen years.
Young Man Why?
Wife (*simply*) I love him.
Young Woman Why?
Wife I saw ... something in him, something fine ... like looking up into the night sky and seeing a star, far out in the sky.
Young Woman Stars are cold, hard, unfeeling.
Wife ...something I could love into being, fan into flame.
Young Man And did you?

Young Woman shakes her head at him. Young Man rises and walks C *where he stands facing* US, *taking in his new surroundings. Wife has not heard him and snuggles the bed cover round her*

Wife Anyway, he had the cutest little bum. And the nape of his neck. Oh!

Young Man turns to face DS. *The first day of his first job. But he is a very*

different young man this time: clever, calm, controlled, and oh so cool. This
young man could one day rule the world. He straightens his tie and slicks
back his hair

Young Woman What's it like?
Wife Mm?
Young Woman Getting married?

Wife gets up. Together they fold away the sheet

Wife I don't remember. Too on edge. Will he, won't he? Be there … be
    faithful … be happy…
Young Woman Make you happy?
Wife No. I never thought of that.

Amazed at her selflessness, Young Woman turns away. She notices a wedding
photo and picks it up

Five years on, you pick up a photo of the happy pair and you don't
recognize either of them. Especially the bride. (*She takes the photo and*
stares at it long and hard)
Manager It would have been all right if it hadn't been for the pressure at
work——

Young Man knocks and enters the office, the following dialogue goes
dizzyingly fast

Young Man I'm your new——
Manager Congratulations, my boy. Executive Oficer, eh? How does it feel?
    (*He rises*)
Young Man Wonderful. Really, it's——
Manager Good, good.
Young Man …so wonderful to be earning my own keep…
Manager You'll start out there. (*He starts to move above the desk*)
Young Man …really paying my way…
Old Man At the bottom.
Young Man …start at the bottom… (*He starts to move below the desk*)
Old Man And what a very attractive bottom it is.
Young Man Eh?
Manager (*reaching to his forehead*) Joke. Must be. Some kind of…
Young Man Actually, I've got an idea.
Manager To save money? (*He comes to the chair in front of the desk*)
Young Man Yes.

Manager Time?
Young Man Yes.
Manager Staff?
Young Man Yes.
Manager Too soon.

Young Man starts to move behind the desk

Young Man Actually, I'm on APS:Accelerated Promotion Scheme.
Manager And your idea?
Young Man To computerize...
Manager It's been done.
Young Man ...middle management.
Manager *(the penny takes a while to drop)* Me.
Young Man I thought I'd call it Rationalisation.
Manager There's nothing rational about me!
Young Man All management staff—below a certain level—will be self-employed, brought in on a consultancy basis, as and when required——
Manager Part-time? I can't survive part-time. *(He sits heavily on the chair in front of the desk)*
Young Man Generous rates. Guaranteed minimum. With bonuses. *(He sits lightly in the chair behind the desk)*
Manager What will I do with the rest of my time?
Young Man Spend it with your family?

Manager rises

Manager I haven't got a family.

Young Man rises

Young Man Get one.
Manager Good. *(He leaves the office)*

Young Man sits at his desk and gets to work. He picks up all the files, tuts and drops them in the bin, then opens up his laptop. While Manager struggles to put on his coat, Wife puts the wedding photo on the fireplace for a change, then Young Woman helps Wife to turn the sofa back to its original position— but they only get halfway

Young Woman No, what I meant was, what's it like *being* married?
Wife It's like sharing your bed with a red hot limpet who commandeers three quarters of the mattress—and the duvet—while you cling desperately to

the very edge. You freeze and he sweats. Halfway through the night, when you've just sunk into unconsciousness beneath six inches of permafrost, he wakes up, flings the bedding on the floor, complains he's far too hot and insists that you—you, please note—should get up and open a window to let in the rest of the Siberian gale—on to *your* side of the room. Then he screws himself into a tiny ball with his bottom stuck right over your side. And starts to snore. Not a gentle snore—with a regular rhythm you can half-pretend is a lullaby, oh no. You suddenly find you're in a pigsty with one little piggy going snortle, snortle, another little piggy going snuff, snuff. Total, blissful silence from the third piggy-wiggy. Till the fourth little porker breaks out with a trumpet blast. At that point, you realize, your feet are like slabs of ice. His are like red hot irons. You think, I'll have a bit of that heat. So you stretch out, and very gently, ever so carefully, place your cold feet on his hot feet and he jumps and kicks and then it's like having a mule in the bed. And thus, more stunned than asleep, you finally close your stinging eyes, in a coma of exhaustion … when the alarm goes off. It's time to get up. Only you can't, 'cos you're frozen stiff and your joints have locked and your head's splitting open. So, take your choice, love. Sleeping with a man's like sleeping with a limpet, a pig, or a mule. And sometimes, all three.

Using his key, Man opens the door to his flat, DLC, *and enters, grumpily*

Man Where's me tea?
Wife "Oh, I do like your hair. What sort of day have you had, love?"
Man Bloody awful. (*He slumps down on the sofa*)

Wife and Young Woman meet behind the sofa and look down on him

Wife Marriage is getting used to personal habits you never thought to see outside a zoo. (*She crosses to the door to see her young friend out*)
Young Woman No. Really.

Young Man rises, turns, and is back home. He takes the kettle URC *and fills it*

Wife (*sighing*) You give and give until giving's all you know. Until he says, "What do *you* fancy doing for a change?" … and you don't know any more.
Young Woman Right. (*She crosses the hall to her own apartment. She uses her key to get in*)

Her Young Man is already home, putting on the kettle. He turns to see her, then comes round the table and gives her a squeeze

Young Man Hi, gel!

Young Woman Sod off!

Young Woman exits angrily UR *to get their meal out of the microwave*

Young Man shrugs and lays the table. Wife continues folding the throw-over

Wife Bad day?
Man Leave that. You come and sit down.
Wife Coffee?
Man I'll make it. Later.

She comes to the sofa and sits beside him, studying him carefully. Pause

I like your hair.
Wife It *was* a bad day. (*Pause*) What's wrong?
Man The job. No. Me. (*He rises and breaks away towards* DC) I'm sorry,
love. You deserved a better husband than me.
Wife Every wife does.
Man What? (*He tries to work this out*) This is no time for silly jokes.
Wife Who's joking? (*She is very concerned. She rises and comes behind him
to hug him*) What is it?

He turns to face her

Man I want to make it up to you, to make it right.
Wife How?
Man I thought we might go on holiday, a sort of second honeymoon ... try
again. If you'll have me...?
Wife I'll have you.

They embrace

Coffee?
Man Yes, please.

*Good, that's sorted. Everything's back to normal. He crosses to the sofa, sits
centre of it and picks up the paper. She sighs. Typical! Everything really is
back to normal. She walks via* LC *to her kitchen* UL

Anything I can do?
Wife You could shift that sofa.

Wife exits to her kitchen UL

Young Woman enters UR, *carrying a bowl of macaroni cheese. She sits* R *of the table*

Young Man sits above the table. She begins to serve a sticky version of macaroni cheese. Man begins to shift the sofa back to the position it occupied at the opening of the play. And in doing so, he has a heart attack and falls on to the centre of the sofa. Old Woman pushes the pram to DRC. *Man rises*

Man And that's where you came in.
Old Woman And you went out.

Lights on cyc change to a deep sky-blue

Wife enters UL, *sees the body (where it would have been) on the sofa, reacts, then freezes,* ULC

Man is about to take a step toward her when suddenly and briskly, Old Man as Doctor and Young Woman as Nurse walk towards each other, C, *and nod in cool, professional acknowledgment of each other's presence. (Alternatively, this section can be played by Young Man and Young Woman,* RC, *in front of the table)*

Young Woman Doctor.
Old Man Nurse.

They stand back to back, apparently addressing different patients

     I'm so——
Nurse Happy for you.
Doctor —sorry to say——
Nurse Good news.
Doctor Bad news, I'm afraid.
Nurse Your wife.
Doctor Your husband——
Nurse Has had her baby.
Doctor —had a heart attack and——
Nurse Mother and baby are fine.
Doctor —died a few minutes ago.
Nurse Gave birth to a fine baby boy.
Doctor My deepest——
Nurse Congratulations.
Doctor Condolences.
Man But I'm not a father. I never had a baby boy.

Doctor Nurse.
Nurse Doctor.

They march to UC *where Old Man gets back into the wheelchair and Young Woman stands behind it. They freeze. Old Woman pushes her pram* DRC

Man But—I never had a baby.
Old Woman No. But you did have a heart attack.

Man crosses above the sofa, round behind his wife

Man A few minutes ago.
Old Woman By your watch. By mine, a few minutes ago, you were born.

He turns toward C

Man I don't——
Old Woman Would you like to see? (*She lifts a shawl or baby blanket out of the pram then, in full view of the audience, flaps it to show it is empty then curls it into a cone shape. It thus becomes a baby*)

Reluctantly, Man comes to DRC

Man That's me? (*He holds the baby*)

Old Woman watches him

Old Woman In my day, when a birth was due—or a death—people didn't bother with a doctor. They sent for me. For a lying-in, or a laying-out, every village had someone like me. Nowadays, people don't like to get their hands dirty, either end, so they send their relatives to hospital to be sanitised into this world. And out of it. But in those days, they had more respect for birth, and death, and people like me. It's a role I played so well in that life, I suppose, I simply carried on with it in this.
Man You're my guardian angel!
Old Woman (*flattered*) Don't be soppy.
Man Sorry. It must be babies. They make you feel all gooey.
Old Woman You won't feel that in a few nappies' time. Give him here. There's nothing sentimental about birth—or death. They're facts. Of life. Crisp and clean and even. Gifts. The greatest we possess. Almost. There. (*She rearranges its shawl then hands the baby back*)
Man What?
Old Woman Speak. And be quick about it. Give him your gift.

Man What gift?

Old Woman The gift without which no birth or death has any meaning. Give him the words that will help him grow, whole and healed. Tell him. Tell your new-born self how to grow.

Pause

Man I... You were born in love to grow in love until to love we all return. Grow, straight and strong and true. Till we meet again. (*He kisses the child's forehead*)

Old Woman sniffs. Young Woman pushes Old Man in his wheelchair to C— *he is now frightened, frail and nearly blind*

Old Woman Now you've started me off.

Old Man Fine words.

Man Who's he?

Old Woman You. (*She collects the pram*)

Man Me?

Old Man I wish I'd heard those words, when I was young. Sitting here, in the evening, before the lights go on, I sometimes think I hear those words...

Old Woman He's you as an old man. (*She turns away and pushes the pram towards* DRC)

Man But I never had the chance to grow old.

Old Woman Humour him.

Very awkwardly, Man crosses C *to Old Man*

Man There, there.

Young Woman goes DLC *and returns with the bench*

Old Woman Oh, for goodness sake. You can do better than that. Sit. And sit still.

Man crosses behind Old Man and round to the bench. He sits, feeling very awkward, especially with a baby still in his arms

Old Woman exits DR *with the pram*

Young Woman returns to her kitchen, where Young Man embraces and comforts her. Woman, seeing them embrace, suddenly feels cold and hugs herself. Through the next scene, she watches them and they watch Man

Old Man I've not been a good man.
Man No.
Old Man Not a great man.
Man No.
Old Man I'm not rich or famous.
Man Doesn't matter.
Old Man No? Good.
Man You've done your best.
Old Man Not really. I'm afraid I've hurt a lot of people.
Man You ... life dealt you a raw deal.
Old Man Not really. I wasted so many chances, you see.
Man No, no. Well, some. A few. Quite a few.
Old Man Frittered my life away. Talents, too.
Man It's not too late.

Old Woman enters DR, *carrying a pile of seven or eight typewritten scripts.*
She has clearly been listening all the time

Old Woman It is. You're dead, remember. This is only "might have been"—
"would have been"—if you hadn't worked and smoked and drunk yourself
to an early grave.
Man (*to Old Woman*) Then what's the point?
Old Man (*thinking the question is addressed to him*) The point? I thought
I knew. Even now, I keep—almost—catching it—like a hat in a high wind,
then the leaves rustle, I turn and lose it.
Man (*rising*) I can't... (*He means "...stand it"*)
Old Man (*panicking*) Don't! Don't close the curtains! Not yet! Please!
Man I won't. (*He sits and takes Old Man's hand in his*)
Old Man I want to cling on to the last drop of light.
Man Why? Why bother?
Old Woman Why does the last leaf cling on to the last branch in autumn?
Old Man I'm afraid—afraid I'll fall into that dark hole below. Sometimes
I feel its cold dampness numb my heart. Aren't you? Afraid?
Man (*thinking about it*) No. It's not frightening. It's not that sort of dark.
More like...
Old Man I was always afraid of the dark.
Man ...like a child...
Old Man Leave the light on!
Man ...snuggling down into the warm velvet shadows.
Old Man Yes?
Man It's more ... that sort of dark.
Old Man I would not be afraid of the darkness of a child.
Man And like a child you don't *let* go so much as *reach out.*

*Old Man does this ... and dies, happily. Woman comes and folds Old Man's
arms back into the wheelchair, then pushes the wheelchair to the table, their
backs to the audience. Old Woman dumps the scripts on the kitchen table*

Old Woman That's the hardest part. Learning to let go. You helped him.
Thank you. Jane* (**use Woman's real name*), could you share these out
for me?

Man I helped myself.

Old Woman We all do that.

Young Woman What are they?

Woman Scripts. For tomorrow.

Man I made an awful mess of things.

Old Woman begins to approach him

Old Woman (*matter of factly*) Yes.

Man Perhaps in the next life.

Old Woman Perhaps.

Young Woman Well, I hope I get a better part than today.

Young Man Whose life is it, tomorrow?

Woman Some woman.

Young Woman About time.

Woman Young, attractive, vivacious.

Young Woman Me! At last!

Old Man I wouldn't get too excited, dear. She's bound to have some man
around to screw it up.

Young Woman At least I'll get to play a heroine.

Old Man Did no-one ever tell you? The best part in any play is never the
hero—always the villain.

Old Woman (*turning back to the "actors"*) Can you keep quiet over there?
I haven't finished with this one yet.

Man holds out the baby, but she ignores this

Man (*rising*) Where now? Heaven?

*Old Woman laughs and the rest of the cast laugh with her. It is gentle, loving
laughter, for they are used to meeting his reaction. He will learn. Woman sits
on the US end of the table and hands out the scripts of the next Life they are
to act out. They have now lost interest in our Man*

Old Woman Heaven's a place for butterflies. Not caterpillars. (*She looks at
him, considers, then smiles*) Heaven's where those who had no chance

before will have their chance, and those who've had their chance—(*she indicates the other actors*)—will help them.

The four actors round the table turn and smile at him, then turn quickly back, for they have something much more exciting and important to do now. It is time for them to find out what parts they will be playing next. They are a group of friends now, united in that buzz of excitement all actors feel at seeing a new script for the first time

Not for you. Not yet. You're still too cocooned in your own story. There are still so many hurts to be healed, wrongs to be righted in your own life before *you* can wing your way there. But I'll watch over you in your chrysalis, keep you safe till you're ready to shed your own concerns and eager to turn outward, fly upward, ready to help, ready to hear——

The other actors point to the scripts they carry

Young Woman —my story.
Woman —our story.
Old Man (*rising*) —the story.

They begin to wander towards the exit RC, *Old Man leading the way, then Woman and Young Woman side by side, Young Man bringing up the rear*

Old Woman (*very matter of factly*) But, you've made a start. Learnt to accept yourself, to love yourself. You've already begun to grow...
Man (*realizing it*) Yes. (*He looks down at the baby and cradles it in his arms*)

Young Man—the last of the other actors to leave the stage—turns to wave to Old Woman. She waves back and begins to cross to the table. Man is lost in thought. Young Man calls over to him, in a friendly way

Young Man Till we meet again.

Young Man exits swiftly RC

Man turns and realizes they have gone. Old Woman collects up the spare scripts from the table

Begin a gentle cross-fade, taking out the general cover lighting and bringing up a pin-spot C. *Man begins to walk into the spot*

Man Where've they all gone?

Old Woman Back. Where they came from.

Man I never thanked them.

Old Woman (*turning to him, with a smile*) No-one ever does. (*She walks on to* DRC, *carrying the remaining scripts*)

Man I'm ready now. (*But he isn't. He's still very nervous*)

Old Woman smiles, but only to herself, as she exits briskly DR

Wait! Nana?

Old Woman (*off*) What now, child?

Man I still don't know … the colour of your eyes.

Old Woman (*amused*) No, no, you don't. Not yet.

Man is left holding the baby. Silhouetted against the blue night sky, his face lit by a single pin-spot, he stands, looking hopefully, listening expectantly for what will happen next … as——

—the CURTAIN *falls*

FURNITURE AND PROPERTY LIST

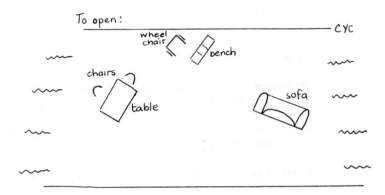

On stage: Table
               2 chairs
               Modern wheelchair
               Low slatted wooden bench
               Sofa
               Large, plain, cotton throw-over
               40 year-old pram
               Shawl or baby blanket

Off stage: 7 or 8 typewritten scripts (**Old Woman**)

WARDROBE

Old Woman: grey knitted pull-on hat, 1930s dress dyed charcoal grey with original floral pattern still just visible

Woman: light grey 3/4 length dress, charcoal grey cardigan

Young Woman: tight black skirt, white blouse

Old Man: black and cream pin-stripe 3-piece suit of 1930s style, pale cream shirt, ancient version of **Young Man**'s tie

Man: black trousers, white shirt, pale grey waistcoat

Young Man: black trousers, white shirt, striped red and grey school tie

LIGHTING PLOT

Property fittings required: nil
1 interior: 4 acting areas. The same throughout

To open: Lights on cyc full amber

Cue 1   **Old Woman**: "I'll get on with the washing-up then."   (Page 12)
          Change lights on cyc to red

Cue 2   **Old Woman**: "Where next?"   (Page 19)
          Change lights on cyc to low level amber

Cue 3   **Young Clerk**: "Not to me, he didn't!"   (Page 32)
          Change lights on cyc to full amber

Cue 4   **Old Woman**: "And you went out."   (Page 40)
          Change lights on cyc to full blue

Cue 5   **Old Woman** collects up scripts from table   (Page 45)
          Begin gentle cross-fade, taking out general cover lighting
            and bringing up pin-spot c *on* **Man**'s *face. Complete by*
            end of play. Leave cyc on full